SYMBOLS, SIGNS &

SIGNETS *by Ernst Lehner*

DOVER PUBLICATIONS, INC · NEW YORK

Published in Canada by General Publishing Company, Ltd., 30
Lesmill Road, Don Mills, Toronto, Ontario.
Published in the United Kingdom by Constable and Company, Ltd.

DOVER *Pictorial Archive* SERIES

Standard Book Number: 486-22241-1
Library of Congress Catalog Card Number: 69-16134
Manufactured in the United States of America
Dover Publications, Inc.
31 East 2nd Street
Mineola, N.Y. 11501

TO HANSI

*in sincere gratitude for her faithful and
unfaltering help and collaboration.*

1

CLASPED HANDS, EARS AND POMEGRANATE
Union, Fertility, Posterity (*Asia Minor*) from J. Bryant's
Analysis of Antient Mythology (*London* 1807)

ACKNOWLEDGMENT

WITH TRUE APPRECIATION for their gracious assistance I wish to thank my many friends and colleagues who helped make this book possible.

My special thanks go to Hofrat Hans Ankwicz-Kleehoven of Vienna, Mr. John Schlepkow of Hamburg, Miss Jeanne Lanty of Paris, Mr. Paul O. Althaus of Zuerich, and Mr. Paul Baratte of London for their conscientious efforts in checking material, names and dates.

Also my gratitude to Mr. Fred Liebesny of New York for making the library of my late friend, Kurt Libesny, available to me; to Mr. Mathias von Mandel of Greenwich, Connecticut, for providing me with valuable Chinese and Japanese material from his Far East collection, to Mr. Ervine Metzl of New York for his encouragement and important contribution and to Miss Ruth Goldberg of New York for her most friendly collaboration.

2

TITULUS (SANCTORUM . . .)
from an old parchment (*Westminster Abbey, London*)

TO THE READER

SELF-EXPRESSION as one of man's most persistent attributes has been studied in detail by anthropologists, psychologists and historians. It is not the purpose of this volume to cover the same ground so amply and ably charted by so many outstanding scholars.

The focus of interest in this study is more special: to trace man's evolution as an artist and designer and to do this through the signs, seals and symbols he has left as his record.

Unfortunately man is a destroyer as well as a creator; and the 60,000 or more prints and the elaborate reference library it has taken the author the better part of a lifetime to assemble were destroyed in a split second by the dynamite charge of a retreating army in the last war. What the author has recreated here has been gathered from materials available outside the war zones; in its compilation he has felt keenly not only the loss of his own collection of data but also the destruction of incalculable hordes of additional material in other private collections, museums, church files, libraries and elsewhere, all destroyed beyond recall by the late war.

The material thus lost included heraldic signs and devices in Austria, Hungary, Poland and West Prussia; religious and ecclesiastical symbols of Eastern churches in Bulgaria, Rumania, Bessarabia and the Ukraine; Hebrew cabala; signs and symbols of the Huns, Avars, Tartars, Mameluks, Saracens and other early invaders of Europe who superimposed their own rites, superstitions, rubrics and sigils on the people indigenous to the lands they conquered.

These losses may be lamented but never restored. If they leave the reader as dissatisfied as they do the author they may serve to help dissuade all of us from incurring any further ravages of future wars.

LIST OF CONTENTS

INTRODUCTION

BEHIND THE veil of Time, primitive man has left a record of himself in symbols he created ages before he learned to write. Just as a child piles up sticks and stones to represent concepts for which he has not yet learned words, so mankind in its childhood built cairns and marked trees in its first efforts of self-expression.

A newcomer in a world in which all other creatures, and Nature herself, were his enemies, man soon enlisted his ability to leave a record of himself in his fight for survival. To his family and tribe the record became a guide to good hunting and better living, a warning against danger, a chart of progress. The disc which represented the sun became, by association, the source of warmth and life. More powerful and more dependable than man it became endowed in man's unfolding imagination with the properties of divinity. The arc representing the moon which unaccountably waxed and waned assumed powers of mysteries it has not completely lost to this day.

Man's rising ability to express himself quickly found—or created—a symbol for each basic concept and occurrence. Because he was still a stranger in a largely hostile and inexplicable world man was both delighted and terrified by his own powers of representation. These twin emotions, hope and fear, which governed his days and disturbed his nights instigated him to create signs and symbols which represented not only physical facts, but all the fancies and supernatural powers he associated with them. Whether they were animate or inanimate made little difference; in his early days man ascribed animism to all things.

Consequently it was inevitable that certain signs and symbols acquired properties of mysticism and magic. The fact that the very ability to inscribe symbols was given to only a few men made their translation into magic that much easier; and this ability gave its owners automatic power over their fellow-men. They could invoke gods and demons; and their amulets, scrolls, sigils, prayer-sticks, masks and other symbol-creating paraphernalia became not only their badges of office but the objects of devotion of the faithful.

―――――――

Because the symbols man has created are almost as multiple and various as man himself neither this nor any other book can honestly pretend to be a complete or exhaustive encyclopedia of such insignia. If, however, it serves the reader as a practical handbook and visual guide through the transformation of simple marks and signs into such elaborate and artistic forms of expression as the emblem, the crest, the coat of arms, etc., it will have served its fundamental purpose. For in the record of these transformations lies the history of all human thought.

ERVINE METZL

symbolic gods and deities

SYMBOLIC GODS AND DEITIES

4

SYMBOLIC GODS AND DEITIES

IN THE INFANT DAYS of human civilization when man banded together to live in groups larger than families, laws and rules for community life were established to keep order inside the growing settlements.

For all happenings around the community which could not be handled by human means supernatural beings had to be invented and these supernatural beings were then saddled with the responsibility for all inexplicable occurrences.

Sun, moon and stars, earth, water and fire, birth, growth and death, rain, harvest and drought, thunder, lightning and storm, all these and other phenomena which nobody could understand or harness became the domain of symbolic gods and mythological deities.

We do not know when and where the mythological beliefs of the vanished polytheistic religions started. The knowledge of these beliefs was lost in the last two millenniums. What we know about them today is of very late vintage. Archeologists began only in the last century to decipher the symbolic recordings on rediscovered brick and stone monuments of Egypt, Babylon, Assyria, Peru, Mexico, North America, and the Pacific Isles. Our contemporary knowledge of the religious symbols and gods in these areas, with the exception of Egypt, is still spotty and mostly guesswork. Our interpretations of the Greek, Roman, and Nordic mythologies and of the centuries-old beliefs of the peoples of the Far East are built on much sounder ground.

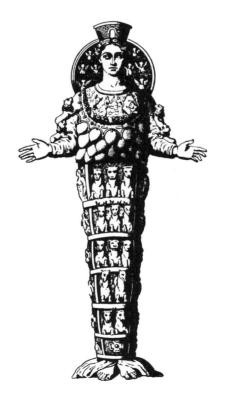

5

6

7

8

9

10

11

12

13

14

15

16

17

18

19

20

21

22

23

24

25

26

27

28

29

30

31

32

33

34

35

36

37

38

39

40

41

42

43

44

45

46

47

48

49

50

51

52

53

54

55

56

57

58   59   60

61   62   63

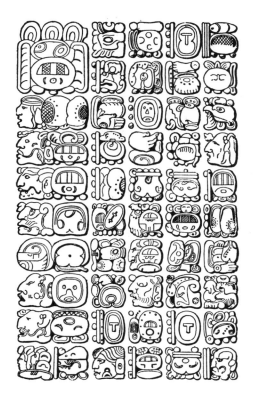

64

65

66

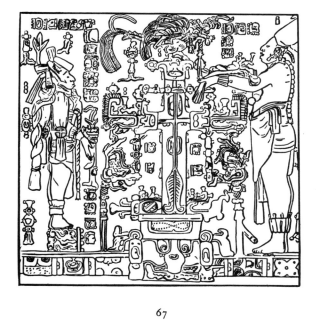

67

68

69

70

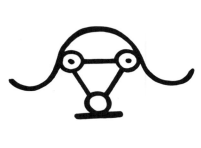

71

72

73

74

75

76

77

78

79

80

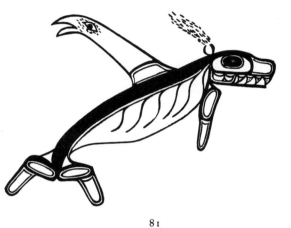

81

82

83

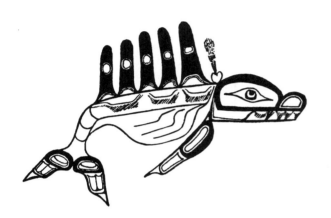

84

85

86

87

88

89

90

91

92

93

94

95

96

97

98

99

100

101   102   103

104   105   106

107

108

109

110

111

112

113

114

115

116

117

118

119

120

魔禮青

121

魔禮紅

122

魔禮海

123

魔禮壽

124

125

126

127

128

129

130

131

132

133

134

135

136

137

138

139

140

141

142

143

144

145

146

Astronomy & Astrology

Cochin Filius inv et Sculpset

147

ASTRONOMY AND ASTROLOGY

GALILEO GALILEI LINCEO FILOSOFO E MATEMATICO DEL SER.mo GRAN DVCA DI TOSC.

148

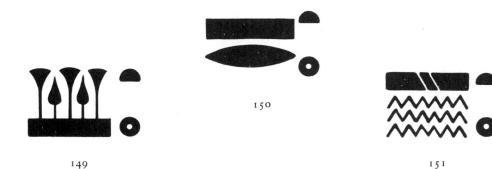

150

149

151

ASTRONOMY AND ASTROLOGY

ASTRONOMY AND ASTROLOGY are the oldest sciences in human culture. The sky, the sun, the moon, the stars, and the constellations have amazed and excited man from time immemorial.

Astronomy is not only the oldest but also the most precise science today. It is almost unbelievable that for over 6000 years the astronomical findings of the star-wise scientist-priests of Mesopotamia, Egypt, Central America and the Far East have stood unchallenged. Their astronomical calendar calculations of 365¼ days a year are still sound today. The only changes throughout the times were in the different divisions of the year into seasons, months and weeks.

We still use today the Assyrian—Babylonian and Egyptian astronomical symbols for sun, moon and stars. Greek and Roman names signify the planets and constellations while the zodiacal signs are Chaldean.

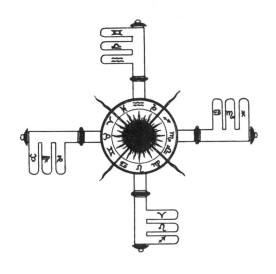

152

153   154   155

156   157   158   159

160   161   162

163   164   165   166

167

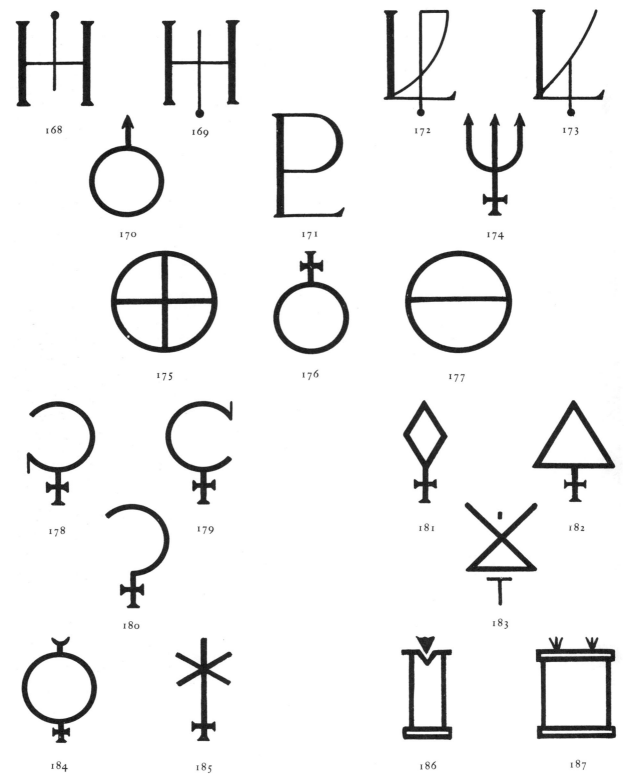

168   169   172   173

170   171   174

175   176   177

178   179   181   182

180   183

184   185   186   187

Ein newer Calender in Cantzelleien schreibstuben, auch sonst in kaufmans und burgerlichen hewsern nutzlich zugebrauchen. Darinnen die zwölf Monat im Jahr in leonen tagen verzeichnet, auch die Ostern oder der Pascha off etlich künig...

Schalt jahren	Folgende Jahren	new Ostern	alt Ostern	Ordnung der zwölff Monaten mit jhrer tagen jnhalt	Tage eines jeden Monats	Tag und nacht er stunden	Tag der wochen
	1594	30 April	31 Mart	I — IANVARIVS Jenner. XXXI.	1 · 17 · 6		Sontag
	1595	26 Mart	16 Mart		2 · 18 · 7		
*	1596	14 April	4 April		3 · 19 · 8 9		Montag
	1597	6 April	27 Mart	II — FEBRVARIVS Hornung. XXVIII.		10	
	1598	22 Mart	12 April		4 · 20 · 11		Dingstag
*	1599	11 April	3 April		5 · 21 · 12		
	1600	2 April	23 Mart	III — MARTIVS Mertz. XXXI.	6 · 22 · 1		
	1601	22 April	12 Mart		7 · 23 · 2 3		Mittwoch
*	1602	7 April	28 Mart			4	
	1603	30 Mart	20 Mart	IIII — APRILIS April. XXX.	8 · 24 · 5		Donerstag
	1604	18 April	8 April		9 · 25 · 6		
*	1605	10 April	31 Mart	V — MAIVS May. XXXI.	10 · 26 · 7 8		Freytag
	1606	26 Mart	16 Mart		11 · 27 · 9		
	1607	15 April	5 April	VI — IVNIVS Brachmonat. XXX	12 · 28 · 10		Sambstag
*	1608	6 April	27 Mart			11	
	1609	19 April	9 April	VII — IVLIVS Hewmonat. XXXI	13 · 29 · 12		
	1610	11 April	1 April		14 · 30 · 1 2		
*	1611	3 April	24 Mart	VIII — AVGVSTVS Augstmonat. XXXI	15 · 31 · 3		
	1612	22 April	12 April		16 · 4		
	1613	7 April	28 Mart	IX — SEPTEMBER Herbstmonat. XXX		5	
*	1614	30 Mart	20 Mart	X — OCTOBER Weinmonat. XXXI			
	1615	19 April	9 April	XI — NOVEMBER Wintermonat. XXX			
	1616	3 April	24 Mart	XII — DECEMBER Christmonat. XXXI			

Nota: In den Schalt Jahren, so mit einem * verzeichnet, hat der Februarius 29 tag. Und ist die summa eines gantzen gemeinen Jahrs 52 wochen, ein tag, die woch sieben tag; macht ein Jahr 365 tag. Der tag mit der nacht 24 stundt; macht ein Jahr 8760 stundt. Zu Cöln truckte Johan by Tonscher.

188

189

191   192

193   194   195

196 197 198 199

200   201

202 203 204 205

206

207

208

209

210

211

212

213

214

215

216

217

218

219

220

221

222

223

224

225

226

227

228

229

230

231

232

233

234

235

236

237

238

239

240

241

242

243

244

245

247

248

249

253

246

250

251

252

256

257

258

254

255

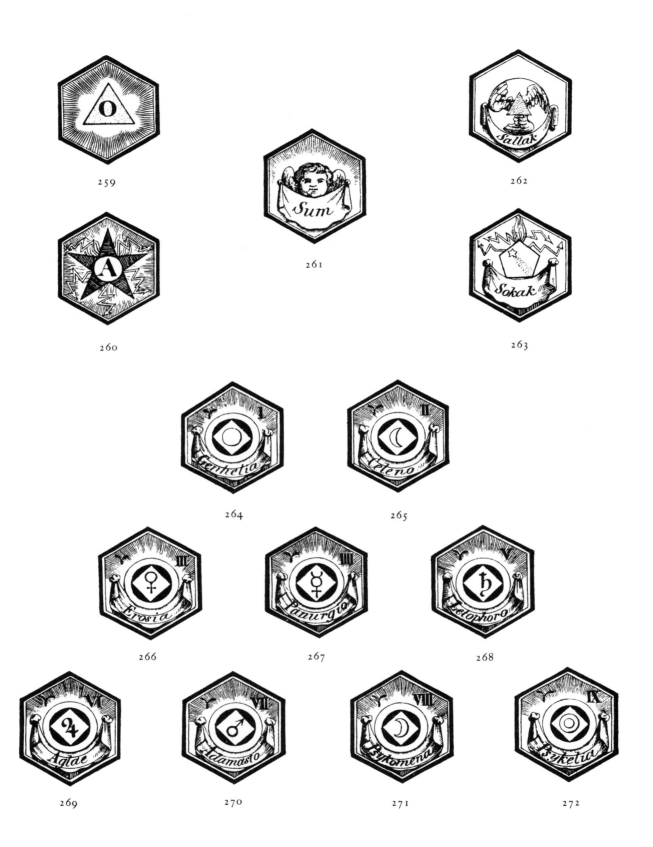

259

261

262

260

263

264

265

266

267

268

269

270

271

272

273

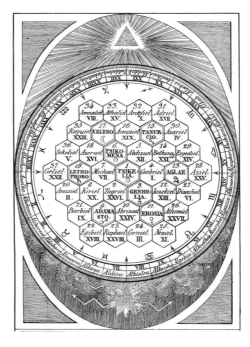

274

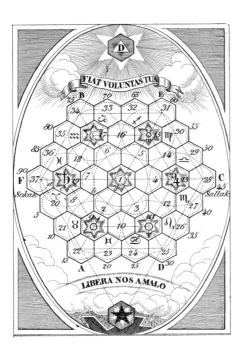

275

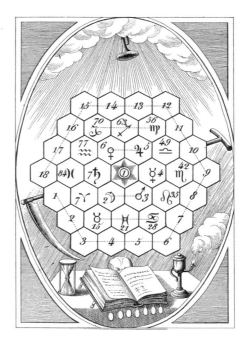

276

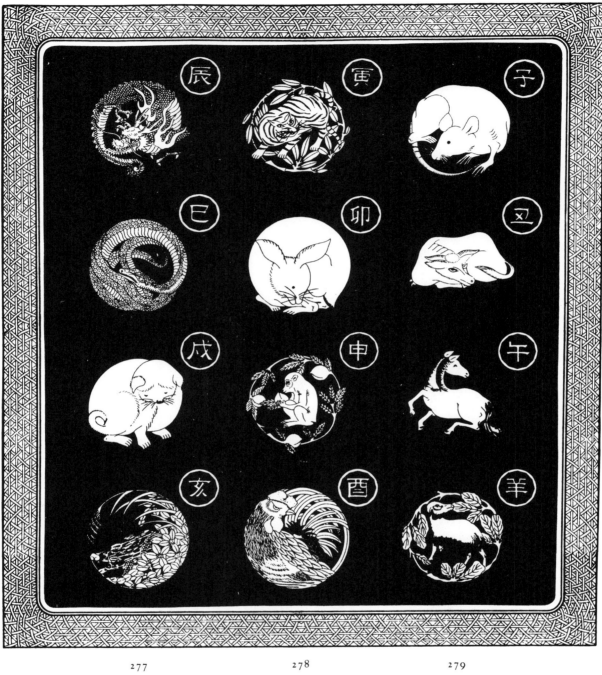

277	278	279
280	281	282
283	284	285
286	287	288

ALCHEMY

ALCHEMY

ALCHEMY

THE ART OF ALCHEMY was handed down through the centuries from Egypt and Arabia to Greece and Rome, and finally to western and central Europe.

The aims of the alchemists were threefold: to find the Stone of Knowledge, to discover the medium of Eternal Youth and Health, and to discover the transmutation of metals. To the medieval alchemist's mind the different metals were but the same original substance in varying degrees of purity. Gold was the purest of all and silver followed closely. All his work was directed toward one goal: the discovery of a method by which the purification of gold could be accomplished.

In the Dark Ages the practice of alchemy was under ban. The church opposed it as a black and satanic art. Rulers suppressed it since they feared that the power of individuals to manufacture an unlimited supply of gold would undermine the fundamentals of their absolutistic reign.

In the early days of alchemy the astronomical signs of the planets were also used as alchemical symbols. Then in the centuries of medieval persecution and suppression every alchemist invented his own secret symbols. Charlatans, quacks, and cheats took over and alchemy became, along with sorcery and witchcraft, the cesspool of fraud and extortion.

In the 18th century scientists tried to pry loose the real achievements in chemistry, pharmacology, and medicine from this nearly inextricable jungle of science, magic, quack medicine, half-knowledge, and plain swindle. At the beginning of the 19th century, John Dalton, an English chemist and physicist, published his chart of atomic elements and created the scientific basis for modern chemistry and pharmacology.

290

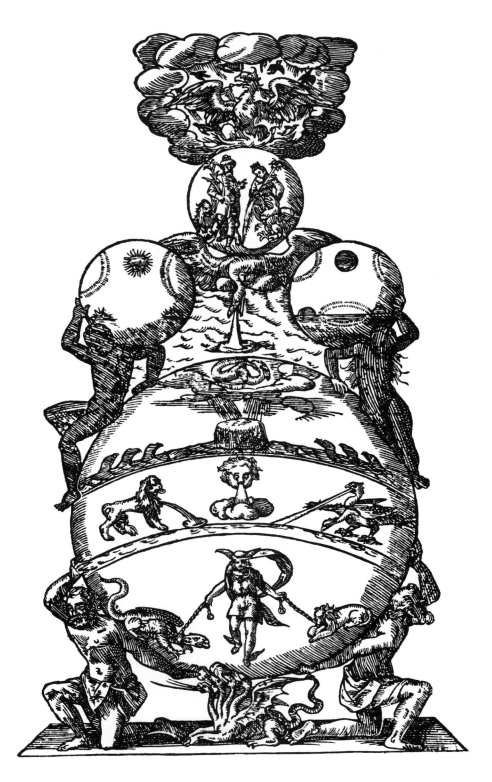

291

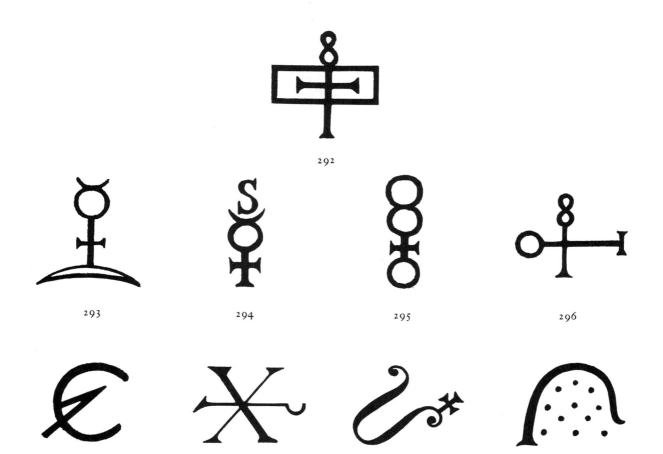

292

293   294   295   296

297   298   299   300

301

302

303

304

305

306

307

308

309

310

311

312

313

314

315

316

317

318

319

320

321

322

323

324

325

326

327

328

329

330

331

332

333

334

335

336

337

338

339

340

341

342

343

344

345

388

346

347

348

349

350

351

352

353

354

355

356

357

358

359

389

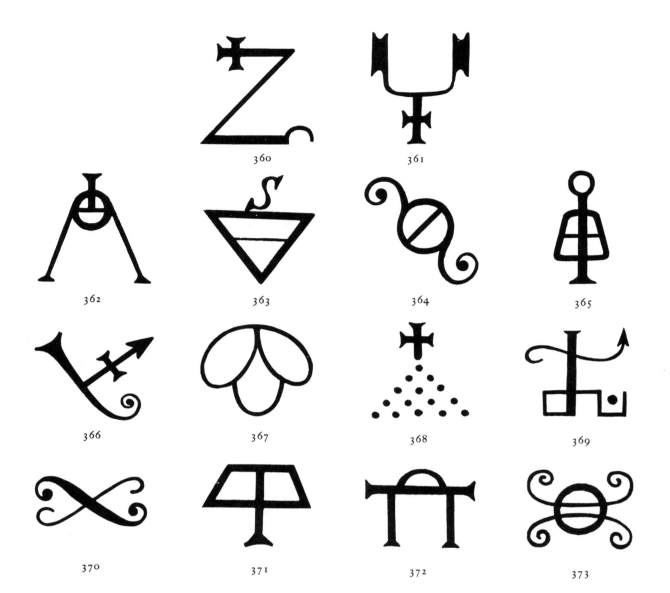

360   361

362   363   364   365

366   367   368   369

370   371   372   373

390

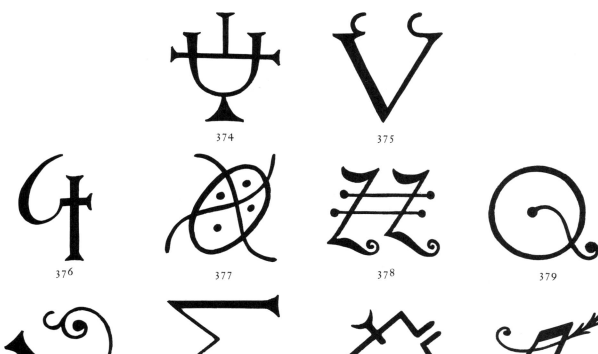

374

375

376

377

378

379

380

381

382

383

384

385

386

387

391

392

393

394

395

396

397

398

399

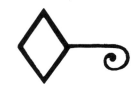

400

401

402

403

404

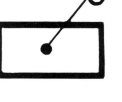

405

406

407

408

409

MAGIC & MYSTIC

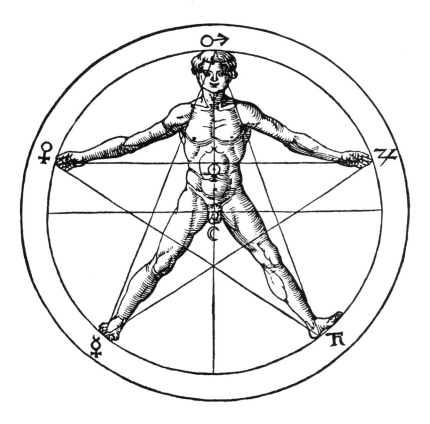

411

412

MAGIC AND MYSTIC

SINCE THE DAWN OF human history man's mind was ruled and dominated by fear and hope of the invisible and impalpable powers behind the phenomena of nature and life, and the inexplicable occurrences around him. He attributed these powers to demons and devils, to angels and good spirits. He invented the weapons of magical and mystical rites and symbols to fight and appease the evil forces and to influence the good ones in his favor.

Rites and symbols of the ancient and oriental polytheistic religions and mythologies, gnostic gems and charms, oracles and mystic signs, Nordic runes, magic circles and amulets all served the same purpose: to exorcise the demons and to entreat the good spirits to give the adept scholar all the desirable things of life and to punish and destroy his enemies.

413

414

415

416

417

418

419

420

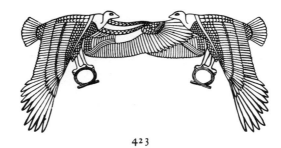

421

422

423

424

425

426

427

428

429

430

431

432

433

434

435

436

437

438

439

440

441

442

443

444

445

446

447

448

449

450

451

452

453

454

455

456

457

458

459

460

461

462

463

464

465

466

467

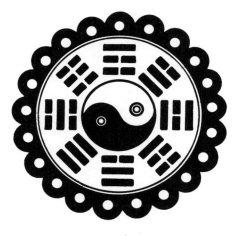

468

469

470

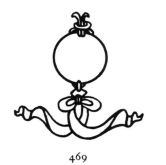

471

472

473

474

475

476

477

478

479

480

481

482

483

484

485

486

487

488

489

490

491

492

493

494

495

496

497

498

499

500

501

502

503

504

505

506

507

508

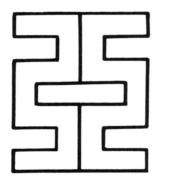

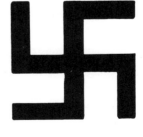

509

510

511

512

513

514

515

516

517

518

519

520

521

522

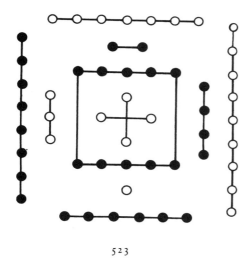

523

524

525

526

527

528

529

530

531

532

533

534

535

536

537

538

539

540

541 542 543

544 545 546 547

548

549

551

550

552

553

554

555

556

557

558

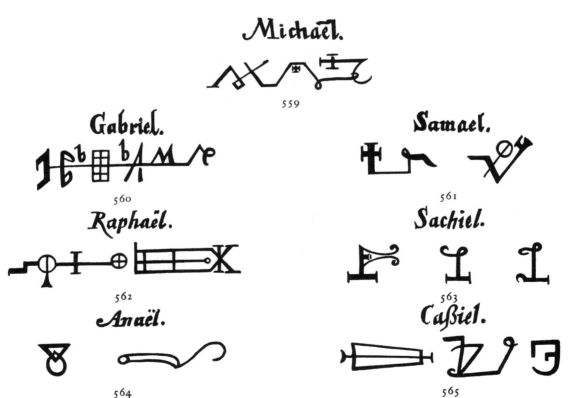

Michaël.

559

Gabriel.

560

Samael.

561

Raphaël.

562

Sachiel.

563

Anaël.

564

Caßiel.

565

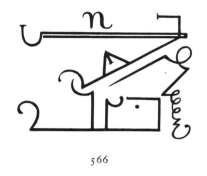

566

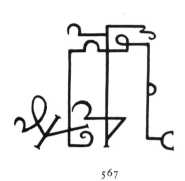

567

568

569   570   571

572   573   574

575

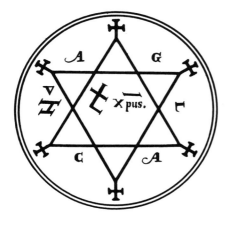

576

577

578

579

580

Church & Religion

581

CHURCH AND RELIGION

582

CHURCH AND RELIGION

THE MONOTHEISTIC CHURCHES make use of religious symbols very sparingly or not at all. Only the Roman Catholic Church has a most extensive system of religious symbols. Through the use of the cross symbol by kings and knights in their crusades against the Islam many hundreds of new designs and shapes of the cross were created. It became an integral part of medieval church and court heraldry as well as the symbol of various orders and distinctions achieved by man.

583

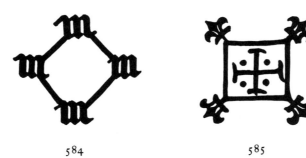

584

585

586

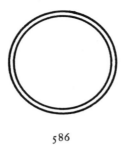

587

588

589

590

591

592

593

594

595

596

597

598

599

600

601

602

603

604

605

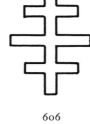

606

607

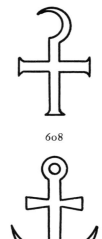

608

609

610

611

612

613

614

615

616

617

618

Church and Religion/SYMBOLS FROM THE CATACOMBS/*page* 110

619

620

621

622

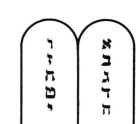

623

624

625

626

627

628

629

630

631

632

633

634

635

636

637

638

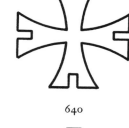

639

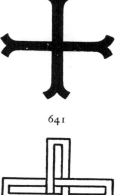

640

641

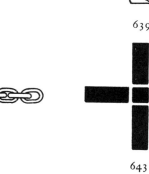

642

643

644

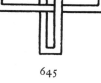

645

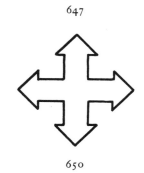

646

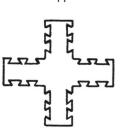

647

648

649

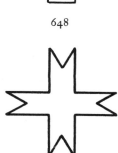

650   651

652

653

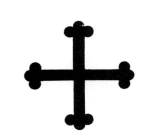

654

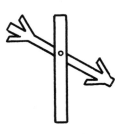

655

656

657

658

659

660

661

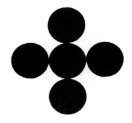

662

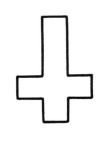

663

664

665

666

667

668

669

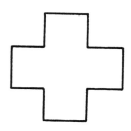

670

671

672

673

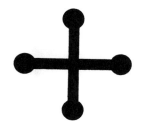

674

675

676

677

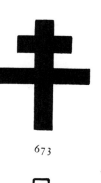

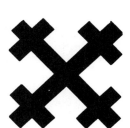

678

679

680

681

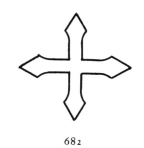

682

683

684

685

686

687

688

689

690

691

692

693

694

695

696

697

698

699

HERALDRY

EXITUS ACTA PROBAT

George Washington

700

HERALDRY

701

702

703

HERALDRY

HERALDRY IS AN OUTGROWTH of the love of medieval rulers and knights for outward distinction, pomp, luxury and splendor.

The designs of armorial bearings were an important part of the artistic expression of medieval taste and the genealogical knowledge of badges, knots, charges, crests, coats of arms, pennons, helmets, and other devices of distinction and family symbols became a science in the early centuries. All the leading artists of that period contributed their creations to this splendid pageantry of the Dark Ages.

Heraldic family symbols and devices are the most elaborate and impressive group of artistic signs. It is not only the multitude of heraldic designs that are so impressive. It is also the accumulation of the artistic skill and ability of generations of artists and craftsmen that we appreciate. We find in heraldry an unlimited sphere of expression throughout an epoch of more than 1000 years.

704

705

706

707

708

709

710

711

712

713

714

715

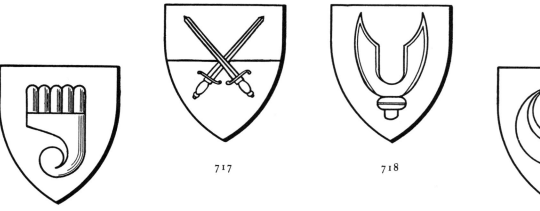

716

717

718

719

720

721

722

723

724

725

726

727

728

729

730

731

732

733

734

735

736

737

738

739

740

741

742

743

744

745

746

747

748

749

751

750

752

753

754

755

756

757

758

759

760

761

762

763

764

765

766

767

768

769

771

770

772

773

774

775

776

777

778

779

780

781

782

783

784

785

786

787

788

789   791   790

792   793

MONSTERS & IMAGINARY FIGURES

795

796

797

MONSTERS AND IMAGINARY FIGURES

OUR ANCESTORS IN BYGONE times blamed their misfortune and good luck, their fears, and hates and hopes on all kinds of invisible beings. To lessen the psychological strain of the unknown that interfered constantly with their lives our forefathers found it wise to give these invisible powers symbolic form no matter how frightful that form might be. They then knew what they were up against.

Crawling and flying beasts of prey, fantastic creatures that were part-human and part-animal arose from the human mind to populate forests and mountains, skies and oceans. Throughout the centuries these creatures were responsible for good and bad happenings in human life, and they had to be fought and bribed, appeased and thanked.

We should not shake our heads over these fantastic superstitions of our ancestors or dispose of them as incredulous. We still are not over that hump today. Even in our modern time too many people outside the jungle and voodoo country still believe in all kinds of animal magic. Werewolves and vampires still roam parts of our planet. Bats are hellbent to fly into women's hair and scalp them. Black cats cross our path to bring misfortune. The sea serpent pops up faithfully every year on the desks of our newspaper editors and gets oceans of printer's ink to splash around in comfortably. But the most horrible of all contemporary monsters is the mouse who still throws womanhood all over the globe into spasmodic fits.

798

799

800

801

802

803

804

805

806

807

808

809

810

811

812

813

814

815

816

817

818

819

820

821

822

823

824

825

827

826

828

Japanese Crests

JAPANESE CRESTS

830   831

JAPANESE CRESTS

CRESTS OR BADGES ARE the expressive form of Japanese heraldry. The family symbol, or *mon*, was known in Japan as early as 900 A.D. and reached its highest development during feudal times.

These crests are all in simple lines, beautifully and artistically designed. Derived from ancient textile patterns, the *mon* is used on everything that belongs to the family, including their clothing. These patterns, woven or embroidered, are worn on each garment in five places: on each sleeve, on each breast, and at the back of the neck. They are omitted only on wedding robes, mourning robes and hara-kiri garments.

The subjects of these symbols are unlimited: animals, birds, insects, butterflies, flowers, petals, vegetables, trees, leaves, armor, tools, accessories, and all kinds of objects of daily living. They are always executed with the subtle feeling for line and space that is so characteristic of the Japanese artist.

832   833   834

835

836

837

838

839

840

841

842

843

844

845

846

847

848

849

850

851

852

853

854

855

856

857

858

859

860

861

862

863

864

865

866

867

868

869

870

871

872

873

874

875

876

877

879

878

880

881

882

883

884

885

886

887

888

889

890

891

892

893

894

895

896

897

898

899

900

901

902

903

904

905

906

907

908

909

910

911

912

913

914

915

916

917

918

919

920

921

922

923

924

925

926

927

928

929

930

931

932

933

934

935

936

937

938

939

940

941

942

943

MARKS & SIGNETS

عبد المجيد خان ابن محمود المظفر دائما

944

MARKS AND SIGNETS

945   946

MARKS AND SIGNETS

IN ANCIENT TIMES symbols, signets, marks and monograms were the prerogatives of gods, deities, and the members of the ruling classes, the kings, priests, generals and other state officials.

Numerous examples of the most fantastic and skillful work of architects, sculptors, painters, scribes and artisans were excavated in the last century from the soil of ancient Chaldea, Babylon, Assyria, Egypt, Greece and Rome. But no names or signatures of the creators of all these artistic works were handed down to us, because actually the creators were only the skilled and educated slaves of their masters. Artwork of every description was signed with the names of the masters, and not of the artists.

In the Middle Ages when artists, artisans and merchants began to break their slave shackles, more and more of their personal signets, marks and names appeared on their work and possessions. Thereafter throughout the centuries the names and marks of stonemasons, sculptors, painters, engravers, goldsmiths, armorers, paper-makers, potters, printers, porcelain manufacturers and so forth began to flow forth on their work in an unending stream until in the last two centuries every human being became the rightful owner of a personal name and signature.

947

948

949

950

951

952

953

954

955

956

957

958

959

960

961

962

963

Marks and Signets/JAPANESE SEALS AND SIGNATURES/*page* 161

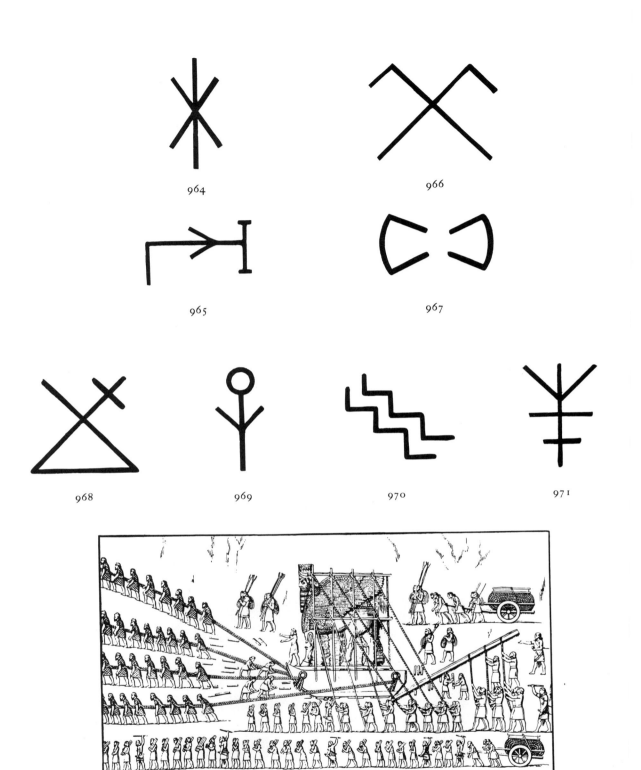

964

966

965

967

968

969

970

971

972

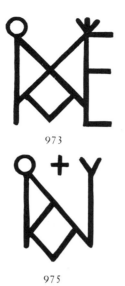

973

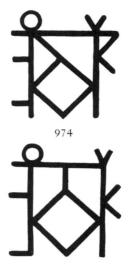

974

975

976

977

978

979

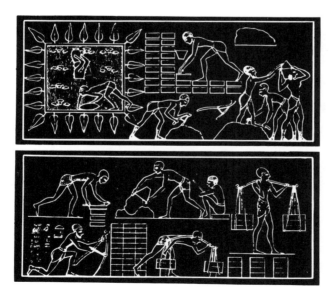

981

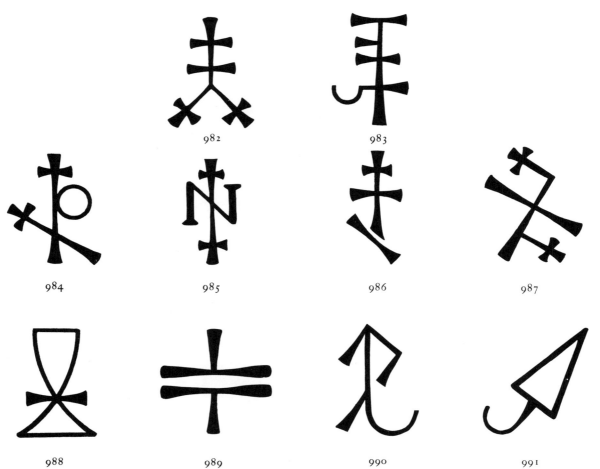

982

983

984

985

986

987

988

989

990

991

992

993

994   995   996   997

998   999   1000

1001

1002

1003

1004

1005

1006

1007

1008

1009

1010

1011

1012

1013

1014

1015

1016

1017

1018

1019

1020

1021

1022

1023

1024

1025

1026

1027

1028

1029

1030

1031

1032

1033

1034

1035

1036

1037

1038

1039

1040

1041

1042

1043

1044

1045

1046

1047

1048

1049

1050

1051

1052

1053

1054

1055

1056

1057

1058

1059

1060

1061

1062

1063

1064

1065

1066

1067

1068

1069

1070

1071

1072

1073

1074

1075

1076

1077

1078

1079

1080

1081

1082

1083

1084

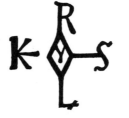

1085

1086

1087

1088

1089

1090

1091

1092

1093

1094

1095

1096

1097

1098

L

1099

1100

1101

1102

1103

1104

1105

1106

1107

1108

1109

1110

1111

1112

1113

1114

1115

1116

1117

1118

1119

1120

1121

1122

1123

1124

1125

1126

1127

1128

1129

1130

1131

1132

1133

1134

1135

1136

1137

1138

1139

1140

1141

1142

1143

1144

1145

1146

1147

1148

1149

1150

1151

1152

1153

1154

1155

1156

1157

1158

1159

KPM

1160

1161

1162

1163

1164

1165

1166

1167

1168

1169

1170

1171

1172

1173

WATERMARKS

1174

WATERMARKS

1175

WATERMARKS

THE TRANSPARENT SIGNS on old paper called watermarks are the impressions of wire figures. In days of old these figures were bent from wire and put on the sieves on which a thin layer of pulp was spread out. They pushed a little water out of the wet paper mass, and when the sheet was finished and dry, a transparent image of these wire figures became visible.

Watermarks are strictly an occidental feature. No oriental papers from the Far East or Arabia ever show signs of this kind. The oldest known watermarks were found on Italian paper made in Bologna and Fabiano at the turn of the 13th century.

It is a fair guess that the possibility of producing these transparent signs on paper was discovered accidentally by some unknown Italian papermaker who may have overlooked a piece of wire on his sieve. Since that time watermarks depicting religious, mystic, and worldly symbols have become common practice in occidental papermaking.

1176

1177

1178

1179

1180

1181

Der Papyrer.

1182

1183

1184

1185

1186

1188

1187

1189

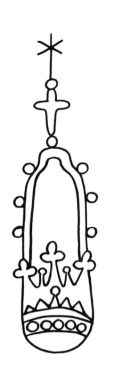

1190

1191

1192

1194

1193

1195

1196

1197

1198

1200

1199

FIN DE
M⚜IOHANNOT
DANNONAY
1779

1201

1202

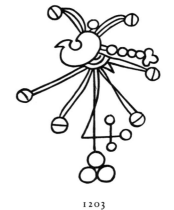

1203

1204

Printer's Marks

1205

PRINTER'S MARKS

PRINTER'S MARKS

FROM THE YEAR 1457, when Johannes Gutenberg's collaborators, Johann Fust and Peter Schoeffer, used the first printer's signet in their "Psalterium" until the end of the 16th century printer's marks are the most artistic samples in the history of trade marks.

The periods of the Incunabula (1457 to 1500), the Renaissance (first half of the 16th century) and the late Renaissance (from the year 1555 to the first decades of the 17th century) were the Golden Age of Printing.

Printers were their own publishers. They belonged to the intellectual and cultural upper class of their time. Many had university educations and academic degrees. No wonder that these artisans were in steady friendly contact with leading scholars and artists and that they used the artistic designs of masters like Ambrosius Holbein, Martin Schoengauer, Hans Holbein, Jr., Albrecht Dürer's pupils and others for their signets.

With the dawn of the 17th century commercial publishers, who were not skilled printers, took over. The printer rapidly became the order-taking accessory to the publishing trade. These publishers were little interested in "wasting" money for artistic designs in front pieces, illustrations and signets or in "wasting" time on quality workmanship in cuts, type, and layout for every new edition. They took whatever they could get at little cost or they copied existing designs with or without the consent of artists and owners. With that unprofessional attitude on the part of this new generation of publishers one of the most artistic periods in the history of the signets came to an early and inglorious end.

1206

1207

1208

1209

1210

1211

1212

1213

1214

1215

1216

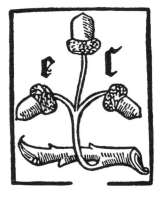

1217

1218

1219

1220

1221

1223

1222

1224

1225

1226

1227

1229

1228

1230

1231

1232

1233

1234

1235

1236

1237

1238

1239

POST·FVNE·RA·VIRTVS

1241

1242

1243

1244

1245

1246

CATTLE BRANDS

DE TAVRO.

1247

CATTLE BRANDS

CATTLE BRANDS

IN THE FIRST HALF of the 16th century the Spanish Conquistadores under HERNAN CORTES and FRANCISCO PIZARRO built an empire from Mexico to Peru. Cattle were shipped in from Spain for breeding in these waste lands, and cattle breeding became a pillar of wealth on this new continent.

The Spaniards brought along the medieval custom of putting their family marks on everything they owned. They branded their cattle with the sign of the breeder. From then on cattle branding became an American heraldry.

The early cattlemen of the last centuries were the rough knights of the frontierless open spaces on the American continent. Their cattle brands are the escutcheons of a trail blazing period.

1248

1249

1251

1250

1252

1253

1254

1255

1256

1257

1258

1259

1260

1261

1262

1263

1264

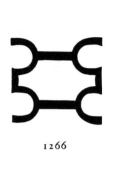

1266

1265

1267

1269

1268

1270

1271

1272

1273

1274

1275

1276

1277

1278

1279

1280

1281

1282

1283

1284

1285

1286

1287

1288

1289

1290

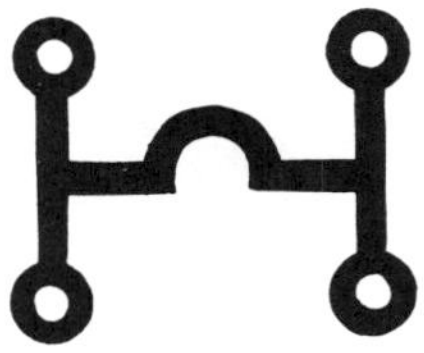

1291

1292

1293

1294

1295

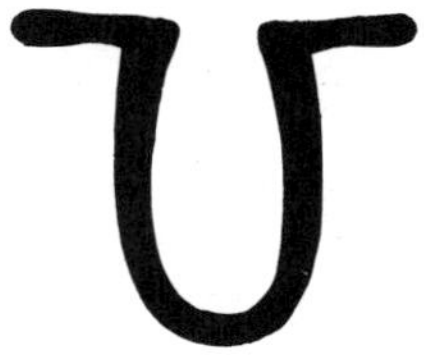

1296

1297

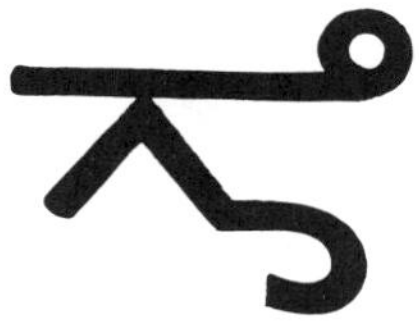

1298

1299

1300

1301

1302

1303

1304

1305

1306

1307

1310

1308

1309

1311

1313

1312

1314

1315

1316

CONCLUSION

IN OUR TIME symbols, signs and signets are still an integral part of our communication system with our fellow men.

The venerable symbols of astronomy, heraldry, occidental religions and oriental mythology are still unchanged today. Scores of new symbols and signs have been added as science, commerce and communications developed new needs for international understanding.

There are drafting symbols and explanatory signs for engineering, architecture, telegraph, telephone, illumination, welding, radio and television. There are weather and map symbols. Signs for railroading and highway traffic. Signals for maritime and air communications. All these symbols are a necessary part of modern every-day living.

The modern business methods of merchants and artisans have developed into the multimillions the trade mark, factory signet and business sign. Other sign and signal codes in constant use are the hand alphabet for the deaf-mute; the Braille alphabet for the blind; Morse, flag and signal codes at sea; symbols for chemistry, mathematics, botany and other sciences. Symbols are also essential in the world of music, dance and color.

It is impossible to review all these modern symbols in this volume. But let us pick out one tidbit from the vast multitude of today's symbols . . . the sign language of a group of contemporary philosophers who live their own leisurely life untouched by the hectic tempo of our success-crazy world—the secret communication symbols of the knights of the road, the hobos.

HOBO SIGNS

1317. IN   1318. OUT   1319. HERE   1320. HALT

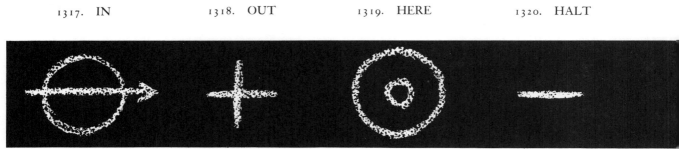

1321. GO   1322. ALL RIGHT   1323. VERY GOOD   1324. DOUBTFUL

1325. DON'T GIVE UP   1326. KEEP QUIET   1327. SPOILED   1328. NOTHING

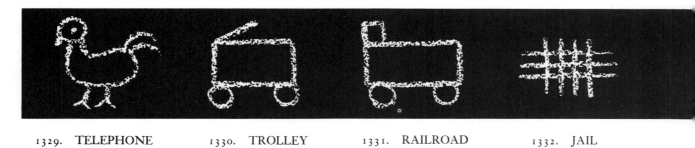

1329. TELEPHONE   1330. TROLLEY   1331. RAILROAD   1332. JAIL

1333. JUDGE   1334. OFFICER   1335. GENTLEMAN   1336. DOCTOR

1337. DOG   1338. WOMAN   1339. WEALTH,   1340. KINDHEARTED WOMAN

1341. YOU MAY CAMP HERE   1342. BE GOOD (RELIGIOUS)   1343. IF SICK, WILL   1344. SAFE CAMP
CARE FOR YOU

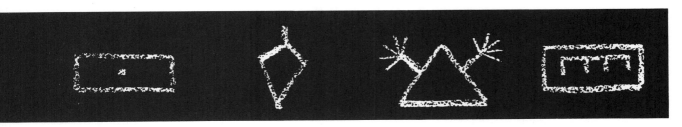

1345. WELL-GUARDED HOUSE   1346. AFRAID   1347. TELL PITIFUL STORY

1348. DANGER   1349. BE PREPARED TO   1350. MAN WITH GUN   1351. BAD DOG
DEFEND YOURSELF

1352. DISHONEST MAN (UNRELIABLE)   1353. UNSAFE PLACE   1354. YOU WILL BE BEATEN.

¹355

AMOR
by Balthasar-Antoine Dunker from Waethard's *"Les Nouvelles de Marguerite,
Reine de Navarre"* (*Bern* 1781)

BIBLIOGRAPHY

ABBOTT, W. H. *Herald Illustrated*. New York, 1897, The Bureau of Heraldry.

ADAM, LEONHARD. *Nordwest—Amerikanische Indianerkunst*. Berlin, 1922, Ernst Wasmuth.

ALLEN, E. A. *The Prehistoric World or Vanished Races*. Cincinnati, 1885, Central Publishing House.

ALLEN, MAUDE REX. *Japanese Art Motives*. Chicago, 1917, A. C. McClurg & Co.

AMMAN, JOST. *Beschreibung aller Stände*. Frankfurt, 1568.

———. *Wappen und Stambuch*. Frankfurt, 1579-1589, Sigmund Feyerabend.

APPERT, G. and H. KINOSHITA. *Ancient Japan*. Tokyo, 1888.

ARCHEOLOGICAL INSTITUTE OF AMERICA. *Mythology of All Races*. Boston, 1925-1932, Marshal Johns Co.

ARMIN, TH. *Das Alte und das Neue Mexico*. Leipzig, 1865, O. Spamer.

ARTIN, PASHA, YAKOUB. *Contribution a l'Étude du Blason en Orient*. London, 1902, B. Quaritch.

BANCROFT, HUBERT HOWE. *The Native Races of the Pacific States of North America*. New York, 1874-1875, D. Appleton & Co.

BAYLEY, HAROLD. *Lost Language of Symbolism*. Philadelphia, 1913, J. B. Lippincott Co.

BEARD, DANIEL C. *The American Boys' Book of Signs, Signals and Symbols*. New York, 1918, J. B. Lippincott Co.

BÉNÉZIT, E. *Dictionnaire Critique et Documentaire des Paintres, Sculpteurs, Dessinateurs et Graveurs*. Paris, 1924, Ernest Gründ.

BERCHEM, EGON VON. *Die Wappenbücher des Deutschen Mittel-Alters*. Basel, 1928, Emil Birkhäuser.

BERJEAU, J. PH. *Early Dutch, German and English Printer's Marks*. London, 1866.

BIRINGUCCIO, VANNOCCIO. *De la Pirotechnia*. Venezia, 1540.

BONOMI, JOSEPH. *Nineveh and its Palaces*. London, 1857, H. G. Bohn.

BOWES, JAMES LORD. *Japanese Marks and Seals*. London, 1882, H. Sothern & Co.

BRIQUET, CHARLES MOÏSE. *Les Filigranes*. Genève, 1907, A. Jullien.

BROCKHAUS, DER GROSSE. Leipzig, F. U. Brockhaus.

BRUNSCHWIG. *Liber de Arte Destilandi de Simplicibus*. Strassburg, 1500, Johann Grüninger.

BRYAN, MICHAEL. *Biographical and Critical Dictionary of Painters and Engravers*. London, 1876, G. Bell & Sons.

BRYANT, JACOB. *Analysis of Antient Mythology*. London, 1807, J. Walker.

BUDGE, SIR E. A. TH WALLIS. *Amulets and Superstition*. London, 1930, Oxford Press.

———. *Egyptian Magic*. London, 1899, Trübner & Co.

BURKHARD, ARTHUR C. *Hans Burgkmair der Ältere*. Berlin, 1932, Klinkhardt & Bierman.

BURTON, WILLIAM AND HOBSON, R. L. *Handbook of Marks on Pottery and Porcelain*. London, 1909, Macmillan & Cie.

BURTY, PHILIPPE. *Chefs-D'Oeuvre of the Industrial Arts*. London, 1869, Cassel, Peter & Galpin.

CALGARY HERALD CO., THE. *North West Brandbook*. Calgary, Alberta, 1900.

CARUS, DR. PAUL. *Chinese Philosophy*. Chicago, 1898, Court Publishing Co.

———. *Chinese Thought*. Chicago, 1907, Court Publishing Co.

CHAFFERS, WILLIAM. *The Collectors Handbook of Marks and Monograms on Pottery and Porcelain*. London, 1893, Reeves & Turner.

CHAMPLIN, JOHN DENISON. *Cyclopedia of Painters and Painting*. New York, 1886, Charles Scribner's Sons.

COLONNA, E. *Materiae Signa*. New York, 1888.

COX, WARREN EARLE. *The Book of Pottery and Porcelain*. New York, 1944, Crown Publishers.

CRATANDER, ANDREAS. Theophyla. Basel, 1527.

CURJEL, HANS. *Die Holzschnitte des Hans Baldung Grien*. München, 1924, Allgemeine Verlagsanstalt.

DELALAIN, P. *Inventaire des Marques Typographiques*. Paris, 1866.

DICCIONARRIO ENCICLOPÉDICO. Buenos Aires, Espasa-Calpe S. A.

DICTIONARY, NEW STANDARD. New York–London, Funk & Wagnalls Co.

DICTIONARY, THE CENTURY. New York, The Century Co.

DOBERER, KURT KARL. *The Goldmakers*. London, 1948, Nicholson & Watson.

DORÉ, HENRY. *Researches into Chinese Superstition*. Shanghai, 1914, T'usewei Printing Press.

DORMÁNDI LASZLO AND JUHÁSZ VILMOS. *Uj Lexikon*. Budapest, 1936, Dante-Pantheon Kiadás.

DRAUDIUS, G. *Discursus Typographicus Experimentalis*. Frankfurt, 1625.

ECK, JOHANN. *Aristotelis Stagyritae*. Augsburg, 1520.

ELEAZAR, RABBI ABRAHAM. *Uraltes Chymisches Werk*. Leipzig, 1760.

EMERSON, ELLEN RUSSEL. *Indian Myths*. Boston, 1884, J. R. Osgood & Co.

ENCICLOPEDIA ITALIANA. Milano, Instituto Giovanni Treccani.

ENCICLOPEDIA POPOLARE, GRANDE. Milano, Casa Editrice Sonsogna.

ENCICLOPEDIA UNIVERSAL ILLUSTRADA. Bilbao–Madrid. Espasa-Calpe S. A.

ENCICLOPÉDIA PORTUGUESA E BRASILIERA, GRANDE. Lisboa–Rio de Janeiro, Editorial Enciclopédia Limitada.

ENCYCLOPAEDIA BRITANNICA. Chicago–London–Toronto, Encyclopaedia Britannica, Inc.

ENCYCLOPAEDIE, WINKLER PRINS ALGEMEENE. Amsterdam–Brussels, Elsevier.

ENCYCLOPEDIA AMERICANA, THE. New York–Chicago, Americana Corporation.

ENCYCLOPEDIA, THE CATHOLIC. New York, Robert Appleton Co.

ENCYCLOPEDIA, THE JEWISH. New York–London, Funk & Wagnalls Co.

ENCYCLOPEDIA, THE UNIVERSAL JEWISH. New York, Universal Jewish Encyclopedia, Inc.

FAIR PUBLISHING COMPANY. *A Century of Texas Cattle Brands*. Fort Worth, 1936.

FAULMANN, KARL. *Das Buch der Schrift*. Wien, 1878, K. & K. Hof & Staatsdruckerei.
———. *Illustrierte Geschichte der Buchdruckerkunst*. Wien, 1882, A. Hartleben.

FORD, G. *Texas Cattle Brands–Texas Centennial Exposition*. Dallas, 1936, Clyde C. Cockrell.

FOX-DAVIES, ARTHUR CHARLES. *Fairbairn's Book of Crests*. Edinburgh, 1892, T. C. & F. C. Jack.

FRÄNGER, WILHELM. *Altdeutsches Bilderbuch*. Leipzig, 1930, H. Stubenrauch.

GAILLARD, LOUIS. *Croix et Swastica en Chine*. Shanghai, 1893, La Mission Catholique.

GALILEI, GALILEO. *Siderius Nuncius*. Pisa, 1610.

GARCES, GORGE A. *Libro de Proveimiento de Tierras, Cuadras, Solares, Aguas, etc., por los Cabildos de la Ciudad de Quinto, 1583-1594*. Quinto, Ecquador, 1941.

GEBER, *De Alchemia*. Strassburg, 1529.

GERLACH, MARTIN. *Das Alte Buch und seine Ausstattung. Die Quelle (Mappe XIII)*. Wien-Leipzig, 1915, Gerlach & Wiedling.

GESNER, KONRAD. *Medici Tigurini Historiae Animalium*. Zürich, 1551-1587, Christian Froschauer.

GESSMANN, G. W. *Die Geheimsymbole der Chemie und Medicine des Mittelalters*. München, 1900, F. C. Hickl.

GOLDSMITH, ELIZABETH EDWARDS. *Ancient Pagan Symbols*. New York, 1929, G. P. Putnam's Sons.
———. *Life Symbols as Related to Sex Symbolism*. New York, 1924, G. P. Putnam's Sons.
———. *Sacred Symbols in Art*. New York, 1912, G. P. Putnam's Sons.

GOLLOB, HEDWIG. *Der Wiener Holzschnitt von 1490-1550*. Wien, 1926, Krystal Verlag.

GONSE, LOUIS. *L'Art Japonais*. Paris, 1886, Maison Quantin.

GRAESSE, J. G. TH. *Führer für Sammler von Porzellan*. Berlin, 1919, R. C. Schmidt & Co.
———. *Kunstgewerbliche Altertümer und Kuriositäten*. Berlin, 1920, R. C. Schmidt & Co.

GRILLOT DE GIVRY, ÉMILE ANGELO. *Witchcraft, Magic, Alchemy*. Boston, 1931, Houghton Mifflin Co.

GROLLIER, CHARLES DE. *Résumé Alphabétique des Marques de Porcelaine*. Paris, 192?, A. Popoff & Cie.

GRUEL, LÉON. *Far Rapport au Chiffre Quatre*. Paris-Bruxelles, 1926, G. Van Gest.
———. *Récherches sur les Origines des Marques Anciennes qui se recontrent dans l'Art et dans l'Industrie du XVe au XIXe Siecle*. Paris, 1926, Librairie Nationale D'Art et D'Histoire.

HANDBUCH DES WISSENS. Leipzig. F. A. Brockhaus.

HAUSENSTEIN, WILHELM. *Rokoko*. München, 1924, R. Piper & Co.

HECK, JOHANN GEORG. *Iconographic Encyclopaedia of Science, Literature and Art*. London-New York, 1857, D. Appleton & Co.

HEITZ, PAUL. *Baseler Büchermarken bis zum Anfang des 17. Jahrhunderts*. Strassburg, 1895.
———. *Elsässische Büchermarken bis zum Anfang des 18. Jahrhunderts*. Strassburg, 1892.

————. *Frankfurter und Mainzer Drucker-und Verleger-Zeichen.* Strassburg, 1896.

HERDER, DER GROSSE. *Freiburg/Br.* Herder & Co.

HEWSON, REV. WILLIAM. *Illustrations of Tracts on the Greek—Egyptian Sun-Dial.* London, 1870, Simpkin & Co.

————. *The Hebrew and Greek Scriptures.* London, 1870, Simpkin & Co.

HIRTH, GEORGE AND RICHARD MUTHER. *Meisterholzschnitte aus Vier Jahrhunderten.* München, 1893.

HOMEYER, KARL GUSTAV. *Die Haus- und Hof-Marken.* Berlin, 1870, Königl. Hofbuchdruckerei.

HONDURAS, REPUBLICA DE. *Matricula de Fierros y Marcas de los Dueños de Ganado Vacuno y Caballar.* Honduras, 1927.

HORNUNG, CLARENCE PEARSON. *Handbook of Designs and Devices.* New York, 1946, Dover Publications.

HOTTEN, JOHN CAMDEN. *A Dictionary of Modern Slang, Cant, and Vulgar Words.* London, 1860.

HUNTER, DARD. *Papermaking Through Eighteen Centuries.* New York, 1930, William Edwin Rudge.

JAPAN GAZETTE, THE. *Peerage of Japan.* Yokohama, 1912.

JASTROW, MORRIS. *The Civilization of Babylonia and Assyria.* Philadelphia, 1915, J. B. Lippincott Co.

JUNG, C. G. *Psychologie und Alchemie.* Zürich, 1944, Rascher & Cie.

KAISERSPERG, GEILER VON. *Buch Granatapfel.* Strassburg, 1510.

KING, CHARLES WILLIAM. *The Gnostics and Their Remains.* London, 1887, Bell & Daldy.

KNACKFUSS, H. *Holbein der Jüngere.* Leipzig, 1896, Velhagen & Klasing.

————. *Dürer.* Leipzig, 1911, Velhagen & Klasing.

KOCH, RUDOLF. *Das Zeichenbuch.* Leipzig, 1936, Insel Verlag.

KOTANY, HEISHICHI. *Japanese Family Crests.* Kyoto, 1915, Honda Ichijiro.

KRAUSE, AUREL. *Die Tlinkit Indianer.* Jena, 1885, Herman Costenoble.

KRISTELLER, DR. PAUL. *Die Italienischen Buchdrucker- und Verleger-Zeichen.* Strassburg, 1893, Paul Heitz.

KUNZ, GEORG FREDERICK. *The Magic of Jewels and Charms.* Philadelphia, 1915, J. B. Lippincott Co.

KURTH, WILLI. *Albrecht Dürers Sämtliche Holzschnitte.* München, 1927, Holbein Verlag.

KUTSCHMANN, TH. *Geschichte der Deutschen Illustration.* Goslar, 1899, F. Jäger.

LAARSS, RICHARD HUMMEL. *Das Buch der Amulette und Talismane.* Leipzig, 1932, Richard Hummel Verlag.

LANGE, R. *Japanische Wappen.* Berlin, 1903, Universitäts Seminar für Orientalische Sprachen VI.

LAROUSSE DU XXe SIÉCLE. Paris, Librairie Larousse.

LAYARD, AUSTEN H. *Discoveries in the Ruines of Nineveh and Babylon.* New York, 1853, G. P. Putnam Sons.

LEE, GORDON AMBROSE. *Some Notes on Japanese Heraldry.* London, 1909, The Japanese Society.

LEXIKON, KNAUR's. Berlin, Th. Knaur Nachfolger.

LEXIKON, MEYERS. Leipzig, Bibliographisches Institut.

LEXIKON, SCHWEIZER. Zürich, Encyclios Verlag.

LIBAVIUS, ANDREAS. *Alchymia Recognita Emen Data et Aucta.* Frankfurt, 1606.

LITTLE GEM BRAND BOOK COMPANY. *Little Gem Brand Book.* Kansas City, 1900.

LUEDE, FRITZ. *Alchemistische und Chemische Zeichen.* Berlin, 1928, Gesellschaft für Geschichte der Pharmazie.

LÜTGENDORFF, WILLIBALD LEO. *Die Geigen-und Lauten-Macher vom Mittelalter bis zur Gegenwart.* Frankfurt, 1904, H. Keller.

McCLATCHIE, THOMAS R. H. *Japanese Heraldry.* Yokohama, 1876, Asiatic Soc. of Japan.

MAGNY, LUDOVIC VISCOMTE DE. *Nobiliaire Universel.* Paris, 1854-1880, Institut. Héraldique.

MANGET, JEAN JACQUES. *Bibliotheca Chemica Curiosa, Mutus Liber in Quo Tamen.* Geneva, 1702.

MANNHARDT, WILHELM EMANUEL JOHANN. *Die Götterwelt der Deutschen und Nordischen Völker.* Berlin, 1860, H. Schindler.

MANTEUFFEL, K. ZOEGE VON. *Der Deutsche Kupferstich.* München, 1922, Hugo Schmidt.

————. *Hans Holbein.* München, 1920, Hugo Schmidt.

MARLOWE, CHRISTOPHER. *The Tragicall History of Life and Death of Doctor Faustus.* London, 1631.

MARNEFFE, ALPHONSE DE. *Les Combinaisons de la Croix et du Triangel Divin dans les Blasons et les Marques de Marchands.* Charleroy, 1939, La Table Ronde.

MEINER, ANNEMARIE. *Das Deutsche Signet.* Leipzig, 1922, H. Schmidt.

MEYER, FRANZ SALES. *Handbuch der Ornamentik.* Leipzig, 1890, E. A. Seemann.

MORIMOTO, TASUKE. *Hayabiki Jomon Kan.* Tokyo, 1881.

MUELLER, NIKLAS. *Glauben, Wissen und Kunst der Alten Hindus.* Mainz, 1822, Florian Kupferberg.

MUENTZ, EUGENE. *A Short History of Tapestry.* London-New York, 1885, Cassel & Co.

——. *Histoire de la Tapisserie.* Paris, 1878-1884, Publi. Périod.

MUNSCH, RENÉ H. *L'Écriture et son Dessin* Paris, 1948, Eyrolles.

MUSPER, THEODOR. *Die Holzschnitte des Petrarka Meisters.* München, 1927, Verlag Münchener Drucke.

MUTHER, RICHARD. *Die Deutsche Buchillustration der Gothik und Frührenaissance* (1460-1530). München, 1884, G. Hirth.

MYLIUS, JOANNES DANIEL. *Philosophia Reformata.* Frankfurt, 1622.

NAGLER, GEORG CASPAR. *Die Monogrammisten.* München, 1879, G. Franz.

NANYO, KYOKAI. *Family Crests.* Tokyo, 1940, South Sea Assoc. Bulletin.

NEW MEXICO, CATTLE BRAND BOARD OF. *Brand Book of the State of New Mexico.* Albuquerque, 1915.

NIEDERHEITMANN, FRIEDERICH. *Cremona.* Leipzig, 1909, C. Merseburger.

NOTT, STANLEY CHARLES. *Chinese Culture in the Arts.* New York, 1946, Chinese Culture Study Group of America.

OKADA, YAZURU. *Japanese Family Crests.* Tokyo, 1941, Japan Tourist Industry Board.

OPPEL, DR. KARL. *Das Land der Pyramiden.* Leipzig, 1868, Otto Spamer.

PALLISER, FANNY BURY. *Historic Devices, Badges and War Cries.* London, 1870, Sampson Low, Son & Marston.

PAVITT, WILLIAM THOMAS AND KATE. *The Book of Talismans, Amulets and Zodiacal Gems.* London, 1914, William Rider & Son.

PETRARCA, FRANCESCO. *Von der Artzney Bayder Glück, des Guten und des Widerwertigen.* Augsburg, 1532.

REINER, IMRE. *Das Buch der Werkzeichen.* St. Gallen, 1945, Zollikofer & Co.

REYMANN, LEONHARD. *Nativität Kalender.* Nürnberg, 1515.

RENOUARD, M. PH. *Les Marques Typographiques Parisiennes des XVe et XVIe Siécle.* Paris, 1928.

RIS-PAQUOT, OSCAR EDMOND. *Dictionnaire Encyclopédique des Marques et Monogrammes.* Paris, 189?, H. Laurens.

ROBERTS, W. *Printer's Marks.* London. 1892, G. Bell & Sons.

ROBSON, THOMAS. *The British Herald.* Sunderland, 1830, Turner & Marwood.

RUTH-SOMMER, HERMANN. *Alte Musikinstrumente.* Berlin, 1916, R. C. Schmidt & Co.

RÜTTENAUER, BENNO. *Aus Cranachs Holzschnitten.* Berlin, 189?, Lehrerhausverein Düsseldorf.

SCHEDEL, HARTMAN. *Liber Cronicarum.* Nürnberg, 1493, A. Koburger.

SCHEIBLE, JOHANN. *Das Kloster, Weltlich und Geistlich.* Stuttgart, 1845-1849.

SCHMIDT, R. W. *Die Technik in der Kunst.* Stuttgart, 1922, Franckhs Technischer Verlag.

SELIGMANN, KURT. *Mirror of Magic.* New York, 1948, Pantheon Books.

SHORT, JOHN THOMAS. *The North Americans of Antiquity.* New York, 1880, Harper & Brothers.

SILVESTRE, L. C. *Marques Typographiques.* Paris, 1853.

SINGER, HANS WOLFGANG. *Albrecht Dürer.* München, 1918, Hugo Schmidt.

——. *Die Kleinmeister.* Bielefeld, 1908, Velhagen & Klasing.

SINGRIENER, HANS. *Vögelin Praktik.* Wien 1534.

SMITH, WILLIAM. *Classical Dictionary.* New York, 1877, Harper & Brothers.

SPENCE, LEWIS. *An Encyclopaedia of Occultism.* New York, 1920, Dodd, Mead & Co.

SPOONER, SHEARJASHUB. *A Biographical and Critical Dictionary of Painters, Engravers. Sculptors and Architects.* New York, 1852. G. P. Putnam Sons.

——. *A Biographical History of the Fine Arts.* Philadelphia, 1873, G. Gebbie.

SQUIER, E. GEORGE. *Peru.* New York, 1877 Harper & Brothers.

STAFFORD, THOMAS ALBERT. *Christian Symbolism in the Evangelical Churches.* New York—Nashville, 1942, Abingdon-Cokesbury Press.

STATE BRAND BOOK PUBLISHING Co. *The Official State Brand Book of Colorado.* Denver, 1894.

STEINHAUSEN, GEORG. *Der Kaufmann in der Deutschen Vergangenheit.* Leipzig, 1899, Eugen Diederichs.

STRÖHL, HUGO GERARD. *Blumen and Blüten in der Japanischen Heraldik.* Wien, 1907, Kunst und Kunsthandwerk X.

——. *Heraldischer Atlas.* Stuttgart, 1899, Julius Hoffmann.

——. *Imitationsfiguren in der Japanischen Heraldik.* Berlin, 1910, Universitäts Seminar für Orientalische Sprachen XIII.

——. *Nihon Moncho, Japanisches Wappenbuch.* Wien, 1906, Anton Schroll & Co.

SWANSON, HARRY R. *Official State Brand Book of Nebraska.* Lincoln, 1934.

THOMPSON, TOMMY. *The A. B. C. of Our Alphabet*. London-New York, 1942, The Studio Publications.

TREITZSAUERWEIN, MARX. *Weiss Kunig* (1516). Wien, 1775.

TSUDA, NORITAKE. *Handbook of Japanese Art*. Tokyo, 1935, The Sanseido Co.

ULSTADT, PHILIP. *De Secretis Naturae*. Paris, 1544.

VESALIUS, ANDREAS. *De Humani Corporis Fabrica et Epitome*. Basel, 1543.

VILLIERS, ELIZABETH. *The Mascot Book*. New York, 1923, Frederick A. Stokes Co.

VINYCOMB, JOHN. *Fictious and Symbolic Creatures in Art*. London, 1906, Chapman & Hall.

VOLKSLEXIKON, DANUBIA. Wien, Danubia Verlag.

WALTHARD, BEAL-LOUIS. *Les Nouvelles de Marguerite, Reine de Navarre*. Bern, 1780-81.

WEBBER, FREDERICK ROTH. *Church Symbolism*. Cleveland, 1927, J. H. Jahsen.

WEBSTER'S NEW INTERNATIONAL DICTIONARY. Springfield, G. & C. Merriam Co.

WILKES, CHARLES. *Exploring Expedition*. New York, 1858, G. P. Putnam Sons.

WILLIAMS, CHARLES ALFRED SPEED. *Outlines of Chinese Symbolism*. Peiping, 1931, Customs College.

WITTE MEMORIAL MUSEUM. Texas Cattle Brands, 1944.

WORRINGER, WILHELM. *Die Altdeutsche Buchillustration*. München, 1921, R. Piper & Co.

WYOMING LIVE STOCK COMMISSIONERS. *Official Brand Book of the State of Wyoming*. Laramie, 1913.

WYOMING STOCK GROWERS ASSOCIATION. *Brand Book*. Cheyenne, 1882.

YAMAGUSHI, H. S. K. *We Japanese*. Miyanoshi-Hakone, 1937, Fujiya Hotel Ltd.

ZAINER, JOHANN. *Buch und Leben des Hochberühmten Fabeldichters Aesopi*. Ulm, 1475.

ZIEBER, EUGENE. *Heraldry in America*. Philadelphia, 1895, Bailley, Banks & Biddle.

ZIMMER, HEINRICH. *Kunstform und Yoga im Indischen Kulturbild*. Berlin, 1926.